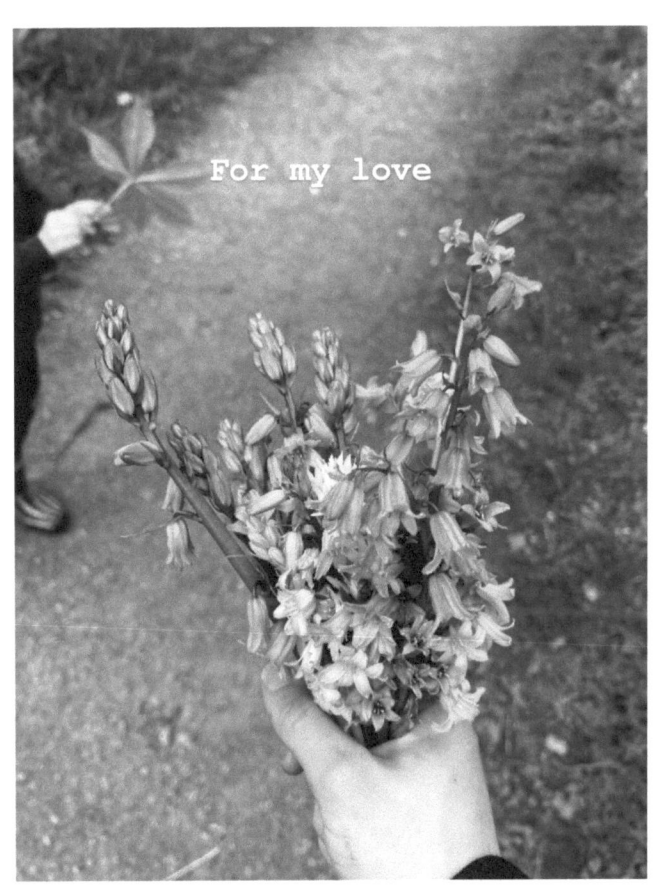

Do not weigh me up against
Earthy desire and heavenly devotion
Contemplated over
Measured up
I will always be wrong
Is there ever such a thing
Good or bad?
Stay in place
Most worthwhile stuff
Packed full of sin
For I do not wait for heaven
Already here
Make the choices
That bring you joy
Do not wait another day

Everything you think I am; I am not

observed absence
unappreciated existence
unfinished, a assumption
empty, a projection
eternally impending
endless possibilities
stories to be written
pictures to be drawn
explanation longed for
categorised desires
lust cravings
ink poured upon
soaked within
the stain of approval
locked to a fate
blend right in

The offering

Take what you want from me
Like the plenty before
Use my resources for free

What you don't understand
Is it takes a lot of strength
To offer a delicate hand

A soft voice to hear
Assume I am meek
When I could roar and cause fear

This gentle and carefree
Fight with art
Dare steal again from me

The Diagnosis

Would it be better to be born not me ?
No inner world to see
I didn't know this was absurd
Voices wanting to be heard
Excitement burns through blood
Turns to panic with a teary flood
Would it be better to not be ?
No fake world to encapsulated me
No shooting stars or fairy dust
Earn eyes and thoughts I can trust
The only world I've ever known
Experienced my way, lived and grown
How can they tell me this is wrong
I was happy with my inner song
If this is sickness's, I don't want to be put right
Conformity brings out the inner fight
I fight with myself, but is it me?
Or does the bitch fight to be free ?

Red wine

Jesus turns water to wine
My eyes turn water to blood
Wash away todays sins
Attempts to clean dirty insides
Poverty reeks on skin
Vulnerable hopelessness
Life threads wear thin
Cry red tears
Drink them up
Wine glass redemption
For one night only

Dragon Bastard

Lay with you
slay for you
keep the treasure
you filthy thieve
Hoards of gold
Never enough
Genetic Protection
No monthly blood diamond
Hours not wasted
Calendar free
Time a good friend
Paid more than she
Invested with returns
Given more easily
In this world
Worth more than me

I Nüwa
your mother
first home
nurturer
lover
shares in blood
hereditary lines
travel
life awaits
estranger
freedom offering
play
learn
suffer
grow
endure
pleasure
pain
paint on your wrinkles

Mona Lisa

Your modern muse
Picture on home Screen
But beneath the locket
Lies something more
Hide your sins
Behind your Mona Lisa
Delete the evidence
I already know
I am not god
I cant be a judge
My own love hurts
It's my fault
I worry awfully much

inner monster

Unborn monster within me
Waiting to know who'll you'll be
I could lose you
My body sick and you were too
Innocence lost with needle in womb
Good news due, come soon
Strength needed to finish the race
A long torture together we face
Imagining all the creatures you to be
Praying born earthside, touch, feel and see
Outcome unknown, stay strong, hold on
Heaven or Earth, where do you belong?
Even if you only stay with me a while
My little boy in my arms, forever in denial

The curse

I felt her there
she stroked my hair
Why did she lay with me
Professing to care for thee
But with cruel intentions
She told me it would be free
If I listen to she
Her voice grew deeper, more mad
Giving in to the offerings she had
To be free from pain
If I agree and don't be vain
What is long hair for or long nails
Ripped faux parts off if all else fails
Unbeautyify to undo the curse
Parts not human but something worst
Paint your face white you are in pain
Life lived walk of shame

Van Gogh at the window

I saw him at the window when in bed
I felt him there as a lay down my head
I liked the man in the hat
Perched on the windsill like a cat
His prencessce did not freighter me
Then crowds showed up, I wanted to flee
Close the curtains, try not see
Hide from birds that perch in the tree
The little birdy told me so
From childhood tales fear it did grow
Who will the birds in my garden tell
Now Granny can't buy what they sell

King

Do you just take?
Drink the juice I make
Hoards inside your head
Keep tied to the bed
You steal my fuel to power you
Underestimate what I do
You can never compare
To the riches I naturally bare
You make your own
For your faux throne

Hourglass Woman

Hands will not win
Grow into irrelevance
Fade to replaceable
Used up
Broken in
Time loop prisoner
Mourned before death
Travelling difficult
Unfollow rhythm laws
Just got started
Victorious Life
Time is not a friend

Butterfly

When all hope was lost
He brought you to me
When all friends gone
You grew by my side
Never alone anymore
Your company needed
As pain grew deeper
And days turned darker
Learning time is fast and slow
In the cocoon you were safe
I a cocoon myself
Unknown days await
Will you fly to the sky ?
Or will wings fail ?
Observing how life is for all
Cruel and unfortunate times
For beings unlike us
This is the cost
For every life
There is an end

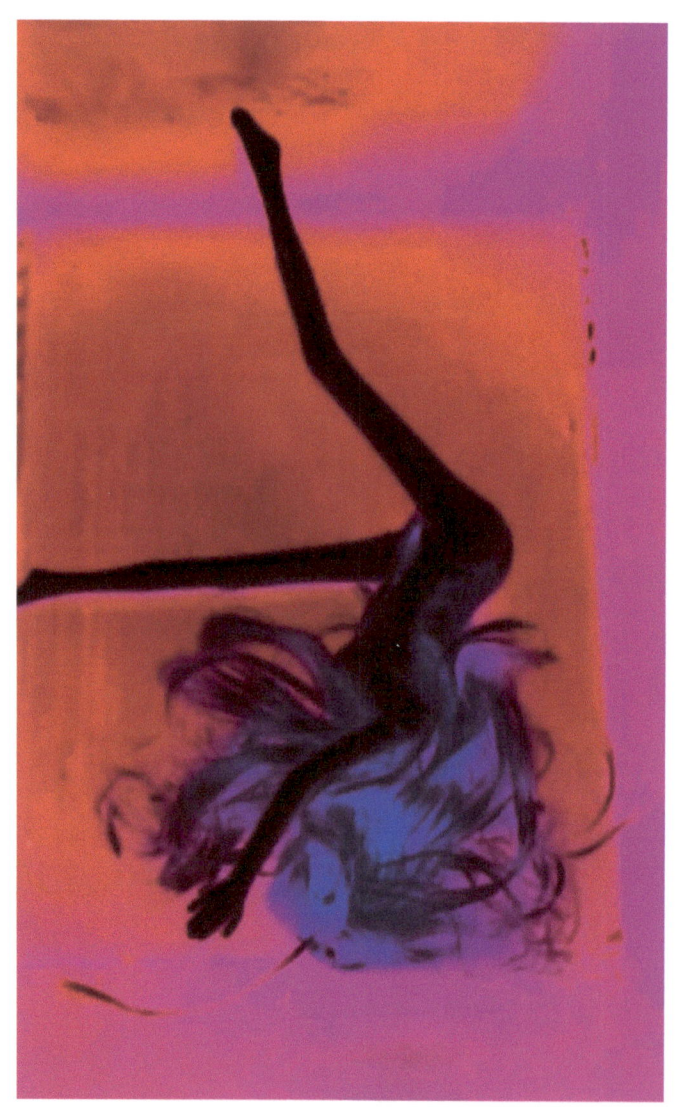

Doll

Undoing stitches
Unraveling thread
Sewed tightly
Knotted in knots
Impossible tangles
Pass the scissors
Cut the rags

Earth Sisters

The heartbeat
Womb Galaxies
Take my light
From sun and moon
Blossom from branches
Nectar from flowers
Fruit from the fields
Lay of my land
Belly full of greed
Drink milk rivers
Bathe in the Waterfall
Indulge in air
Ungrateful breaths
Mining my riches
Lies onto a hand
Scar my skin
Destroying me
Nurturing you

Lonley
Lonley

I know why they listen to the radio
I learnt that already

Let me bring my man

I would share Heras apple with you
To live forever by your side
We could walk hand in hand
Throughout all realities
Through this life and the one after
We could sleep side to side
Not just underneath sheets
But in the clouds
And beneath the earth
Ashes in the wind
Not just conscious
But when dreaming
Restrained together
In boundless love

Vagabond artist

I am without talent
Without a part
Withought the head
Needed for art
Cant work like a dog
But I work like me
Like a wild woman
Wants to be free
I work hard
I work my way
I can't work in one place
I can't stay
With this one life
Freedom to roam
Down different paths
No need for a home
To be enslaved
Like Venus
To the checkouts
To the sweetness
To the thrill
To the phone
Lost in this life
Art the home

My desires

Where are my offerings?
Solely take from me
Like the plenty before
Use my resources for free
Easy, not what they appear to be
What you don't understand
Is it takes a lot of strength
To offer a delicate hand
A soft voice
For you to hear
When I could roar and cause fear
You see it takes a lot to be this meek
This gentle
This carefree
They want to take it from me

Online girls

He went away for a while
Fell for an online girl
Illusions that can be
Anything craved to see
Search box fantasy
Anything asked of them
Wake up alone
You're with new girls on the phone
Leave me in darkness
Screen lights your way
Travel towards the star
A fictional character
I can't compete
I refuse to compare

Open me up
Rip out my heart
Like molten metal
Pour down me
Pick the petals from my flower
One by one

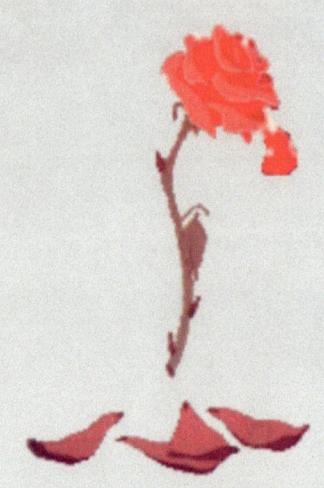

Mad woman

I'll pull the flowers out the dirt
How dare beauty exist
When I hurt
I'll go mad and go crazy
Feel emotions I never had
Snapped in half
She is dragged out of me
Hands round ankles
Pulling feet
Pulling hair
The beast within
Invited out by pain
Pills to lock her up
She exists now
This can't be undone
She is hungry

Redemption

I tried to be a saint for you
For you sinned much
Felt the pressure
Blamed for what I had not done
Punished for your crimes
What has love become?
I was easier than you
To talk down too
Maybe it made them feel in control
The gods know why they hurt me?
Or was it you?

Hot chocolate

I didn't get sober for this
I got sober to live
To do the small mundane things
That I had missed out on
To bake and paint
What made me happy all along
Picnic and walks to the river
Over the styles
Picking wild flowers from fields in between
Hot chocolate in the evening
Memories I know
Love I can feel
But with the good
Comes the bad
Pain cuts deeply
Drown in tears
Suffocating sadnesses
No escape now
Feel life
Feel every part
The way it is supposed to be

Oh come let him adore me

In the dark of the night
Haunting loneliness
Lost in person prayer
Come adore me
Bring me humble gifts
A St Bridgette vision
You supply all the light
No need for a candle
In the dark of the night
You are my Devine light

The flood

Cried for 40 days
Cried for 40 nights
Mascara obsolete
Makeup of tears
Flood season due
Will I make it through
Say my goodbyes
And apologies
Suitcase is packed
Mummy is gone for a while
Sorry my children
Goodbye solid land
Trapped in a vessel
Drifting up and down
Sea sickness
Out of control
Is this time the last ?
In the gods hands now

Miserable old bastard

Paint on your wrinkles
Let your hair go grey
You grow more handsome
In every way
Do not try to cheat life
Why hide behind youth
When you've paid that price
To be young was difficult
Not all that fun
You have learnt lessons
And made your mark
You've carved yourself
Into this part
A book of stories
A museum of experience
A living piece of art
What is more scary than getting old
Is wasting time in the past
For it passes so fast
This gift we have
Vanity is not mortality
Playing the fool to yourself
Whats the point of that

Jewellery clad warrior

Fists full of stones
Gems, flesh and bones
Like armour
Protection and salvation
To gaze down upon
When times are tough
Museum on the body
Of memories gone
Times of love and freedom
That will come again

www.ingramcontent.com/pod-product-compliance
Lightning Source LLC
Chambersburg PA
CBHW051940210526
45473CB00006B/2321